Adventures of an Astronaut

CAROL FALLON

GILL EDUCATION

Contents

Note: 1st Class Readers 1 and 2 cover 18 units of work. For ease of planning, the numbering is consistent with the Skills Book across the two Readers: Reader 1 covers Units 1–9 and Reader 2 covers Units 10–18.

Grandad's Report on School

"Look at this, Ella!" said Mam.

It is the last day of the summer holidays.

It is <u>raining cats and dogs</u> outside.

Mam has a box of Grandad's old things.

There are toys and games inside.

On top is a book with **doodles** on the cover.

1

"It's Grandad's First Class English copy," said Mam.

Ella and Mam open it.

On the first page is a report on school.

"Look at Grandad's **writing**!" said Ella.

They begin to read...

School
by James Mooney

School is a place where children go to learn.

They read, write and do sums.

Sometimes there are games and **treats** too!

In school, children meet lots of other children.

They make **friends**.

Children start school when they are around five years old.

It is a big day.

School Buildings

Schools are small **buildings**.

Sometimes they look like big houses!

They have fireplaces and **chimneys**.

They have big windows.

There are only one or two classrooms.

Many classes share a classroom.

They share a teacher too.

Children's toilets are not in the school building.

They are outside and are called outhouses.

There are girls' toilets and boys' toilets.

Sometimes a wall is used to split up the playground.

There is an area for the boys and an area for the girls.

Schools in towns are bigger than schools in the country.

Most children walk to school.

Classrooms

Class sizes are big.

There can be sixty children in one classroom.

Turf is put on the fire to keep **everyone** warm.

Children take it in turns to bring in turf.

Children sit in lines to look at the blackboard.

The children sitting beside the fire are the warmest.

Pupils sit on a bench behind a desk.

The desk has a lid that lifts up.

There is a **slot** on the desk so pencils won't roll off.

Children have only some books.

They learn from the blackboard.

Schoolwork

In school, children learn how to read, write and do sums.

Children write using pens.

They dip their pen into ink and write in their copies.

It is hard to write without making **smudges**!

Girls learn how to knit.

Maps and posters are hung on the walls.

Teachers

Teachers use blackboards.

They use chalk to write on them.

Teachers call the roll from the roll book.

This is a big book!

Teachers are **strict**.

School is an **important** part of children's lives.

Mam and Ella finish reading.

"Wow," said Ella. "School is not the same now!"

She wanted to show Grandad's copy to her new teacher the next day.

"Can you write a report on what school is like now?" said Mam.

Ella got a pencil and began to write...

Who knows?

In years to come, Ella's grandchildren might be reading what school was like for her!

My First Day

See me skip,

See me run,

I'm going to like everyone.

See me smile,

See me grin,

When the teacher calls me in.

See me work,

See me play,

I'm in school –

Hip hip hooray!

Four Seasons in One Day

2

My reading goal ★ Talk about the meaning of new words.

It is a windy day in autumn.

First Class are on a nature walk with Ms Brady.

They see **leaves** falling.

The sun begins to shine.

Ms Brady puts on her sunglasses.

They are pineapple ones. (She got them on her holidays!)

Ella spots **hedgehogs** playing.

Look at the baby's pink nose!

The weather is cold.

Tom is glad to have his hat.

First Class hunt for acorns. Ella finds a big one!

Soon, it starts to rain.

"It's four **seasons** in one day!" says Ms Brady as they hurry back to school.

On the way, Robbie and Anna have fun jumping over puddles!

At school, everyone puts their leaves and acorns on the nature table.

They hang up their coats.

Ms Brady asks First Class to write a report about a season.

Tom and Robbie work **together**.

Tom likes working with his friend.

Robbie is fun!

When they finish, Ms Brady puts the reports on the wall.

"Wow," she says, "these are **fantastic**!"

Spring

In Ireland, spring starts in February.

Spring lasts until the end of April.

Spring is like pressing a 'restart' button.

It is a time when baby animals are born.

Cows have calves and lambs arrive on farms.

Birds build their nests and have chicks.

Frogs lay **frogspawn**.

In spring, plants begin to grow again.

They need water, sun, heat and soil to grow.

Leaves come back on the trees.

Flowers <u>begin to bloom</u>.

The weather gets warmer.

Days get longer.

There is more time to play outside.

Saint Patrick's Day, Mother's Day and April Fools' Day are in spring.

Spring brings lots of fun days.

Summer

Summer is the warmest time of the year.

May, June and July are the summer months.

Summer is holiday season!

The days are long and warm.

June 21st is the longest day of the year.

People spend more time outside.

Plants grow because of all the sunshine.

People wear T-shirts and shorts.

Sometimes we go to the beach.

(<u>Fingers crossed</u> the sun shines!)

Autumn

Autumn begins in August. It ends in October.

Lots of new **beginnings** happen in autumn.

We go back to school.

We start a new class.

We get a new teacher.

Hallowe'en is in autumn. Everyone can dress up.

The weather gets colder.

Leaves fall from the trees and there are fewer flowers.

The days are shorter.

The nights are longer.

In some places around the world, autumn is known as fall.

Winter

Winter lasts from November until the end of January.

This is the coldest season in Ireland.

The trees are bare and animals **hibernate**.

Flowers stop growing in winter too.

Frost arrives and sometimes it snows.

Everyone wraps up warm.

Christmas and the New Year are **celebrated** in winter.

It is an exciting time of year!

Tom and Robbie are **proud** of their report.

It was fun working as a team.

Tom drew a beach and Robbie drew a crab waving hello!

Can you guess the season?

Ms Brady says the weather in Ireland is "<u>not too hot, not too cold</u>."

"It's just right," says Ella.

"Like Goldilocks would say!" laughs Tom.

Bed in Summer
by Robert Louis Stevenson

In winter I get up at night
And dress by yellow candle light.
In summer, quite the other way,
I have to go to bed by day.

I have to go to bed and see
The birds still hopping on the tree,
Or hear the grown-up people's feet
Still going past me in the street.

And does it not seem hard to you,
When all the sky is clear and blue,
And I should like so much to play,
To have to go to bed by day?

Wild About Wildlife

3

My reading goal ★ Self-correct as I read: Does it look right, sound right and make sense?

Evan, Ella and Tom were playing a game.

It was called 'Anything Else'.

"If you could be anything else, what would you be?" asked Evan.

Ella and Tom had lots of ideas.

A bat, a dog, a fish...

This game was fun!

In the end, they picked wild animals.

Let's take a look.

Evan chose a **spider**.

He liked spiders.

He liked their webs more!

Spiders

A spider has eight legs.

It can have eight eyes too.

A spider has fangs.

A fang is like a long **needle**.

Spiders can be big or small.

They live in lots of places.

Spiders live in trees and under rocks.

They live in houses too!

A spider eats **insects**.

It spins a web.

The spider uses the web to trap the insects.

"If I were a spider, I would make the biggest web ever!" said Evan.

Ella wanted to be a starfish.

She had read about starfish in her new book.

She knew lots about them.

Starfish

A starfish is not a fish.

It is an animal.

Starfish can be called sea stars.

Starfish can be red, orange or yellow.

They have five or more arms.

A starfish doesn't have brains or blood.

It cannot swim.

It has tiny feet all over its body.

These help the starfish move in the water.

A starfish lives in the sea.

It eats **snails** and tiny fish.

Some starfish can change from a boy to a girl.

These are called **cushion** starfish.

"I like being a girl," said Ella.

Tom chose an owl.

"An owl is **wise** and so am I," he said.

Owls

An owl is a bird.

It has big eyes, a flat face and a beak.

An owl has claws to help it hunt.

The **female** owl is bigger than the male owl.

Owls hoot. They also hiss and growl.

They don't make any **noise** when they fly.

Owls live in trees.

They eat insects and small birds.

Sometimes owls eat fish too.

Owls sleep in the daytime.

They are **active** at night.

Barn owls have heart-shaped faces.

"If I were an owl, I'd see all the things that happen at night," said Tom.

Meg and Mel came into the room.

They had been shopping with Mam.

"What would Meg and Mel be?" asked Ella.

"Dad calls Meg and Mel tigers. They keep him <u>on his toes</u>," said Tom.

Tigers

Tigers are wild cats.

They are really big.

They have large paws and claws.

Tigers like to live near water.

Tigers will eat any animal they can catch.

Tigers can run very fast.

They are good swimmers too.

Tigers are orange.

They have black and white **stripes**.

No two tigers have the same set of stripes.

In this way, every tiger is **different**.

Meg and Mel started to fight.

"Look, Meg and Mel are really like tigers now!" said Tom.

"What would you be, Luna?" asked Evan.

"Woof!" said Luna.

"That's <u>as easy as ABC</u>. Luna would be Luna," said Ella.

"The best dog in the world," said Tom.

Our Wildlife

Scuttle like a spider,

Hover like a fly,

Soar like a swallow

High up in the sky.

Snuffle like a badger,

Buzz like a bee,

Scamper like a squirrel

Through the branches of a tree.

Curl up like a hedgehog,

Slither like a snake,

Quack like a duckling

As it swims across the lake.

Creatures all around us

That crawl or swim or fly.

Which is your favourite –

And can you tell me why?

Adventures of an Astronaut

My reading goal ★ Talk about the interesting parts of this report.

Hallowe'en is almost here.

Tom is excited.

Last year he went as a **skeleton.**

Tom's dad painted white bones onto his clothes.

He may have smelled funny, but he looked good!

This year, Tom wants to dress up as an **astronaut**.

An astronaut travels in space.

Do you know any astronauts?

Chris Hadfield is Tom's **favourite**.

He was the first astronaut to send a message in Irish from space.

He posted a photo of Dublin too.

Tom wants to write a report on astronauts.

He watches videos on YouTube with his dad and reads books on space.

Would you like to read what he found out?

Morning in Space

Astronauts are busy.

Every day is planned.

They wake up, eat and brush their teeth. Just like you!

There is one big **difference**.

Everything in space floats because there is less **gravity**.

Gravity keeps you on the ground.

It also causes things to fall.

Taps don't work in space because water would go everywhere.

Water is kept in bags.

Astronauts **squeeze** the bags until a ball of water comes out.

Astronauts use toothpaste to brush their teeth.

When they finish, they don't spit out the toothpaste. They swallow it!

(Don't try this at home.)

Working in Space

Astronauts do tests in space.

They test liquids in space.

They clean the space station.

They go on spacewalks.

They wear special suits to protect them.

Eating in Space

All food is kept in bags.

Food lasts a long time – some can last a year and a half before it goes off!

Astronauts don't eat bread in space.

The crumbs would float everywhere.

It would be hard to clean up.

They use wraps to make **sandwiches** instead.

Exercise in Space

Astronauts work out for two hours a day to stay healthy.

This is an important part of their day.

Exercise helps keep their hearts, lungs and bones strong.

There is a space **treadmill** with straps.

There is also a bike.

This means that astronauts can run and cycle in space.

Free Time in Space

Astronauts spend time looking out the windows.

They take photos of the stars.

They look down at Earth.

They watch movies and listen to music.

They play computer games and read books.

They send emails to their friends.

Once a week, they talk to their family using video.

Sleeping in Space

When it is time to <u>hit the hay</u>, astronauts sleep in pods.

These are tiny bedrooms with sleeping bags tied to the wall.

With less gravity, their bodies relax.

They don't need anything to hold them up, so there is no pillow or bed.

When they sleep, astronauts' arms float up in front of them. Their heads tip forward.

They look like zombies – but nice ones!

Astronauts wear special **pyjamas**.

They may have to get up for space duty in the night.

They try to sleep for eight hours.

They are tired after their long day of work.

Would you like to be an astronaut like Tom?

Climb Aboard the Spaceship!

Climb aboard the spaceship,

We're going to the moon,

Hurry and get ready,

We're going to blast off soon!

Put on your helmets,

And buckle up real tight

Here comes the countdown,

Let's count with all our might!

10–9–8–7–6–5–4–3–2–1 – BLAST OFF!

Tara the Tooth

My reading goal ★ Ask questions before, during and after reading.

5

On Monday night, Ella was in bed at Nana's house.

She <u>felt under the weather</u>.

Her tooth was sore.

Really sore.

Had she brushed it too hard?

Had she had too many sweets?

Nana gave her a book.

She said, "Read this and sleep, Ella. Your tooth will be **better** in the morning."

Ella was **worried**.

She wanted her teeth to be happy.

They helped her to talk and eat.

They looked good too!

She brushed them twice a day.

She ate healthy food to keep them strong... but she also loved sweets!

Ella began to read.

Soon, she fell asleep.

She began to **dream**...

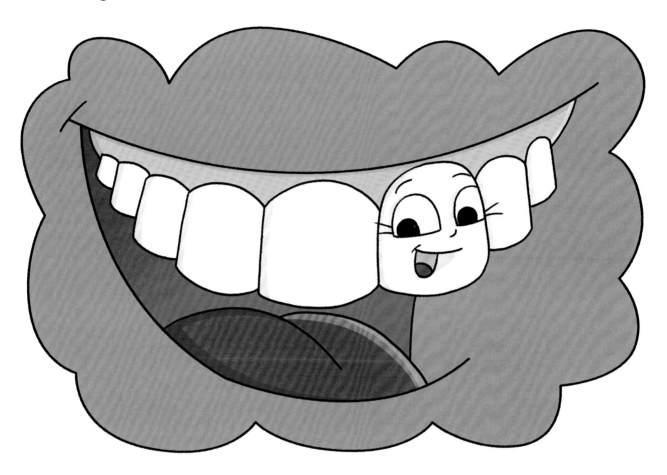

"Hello! I'm Tara, Ella's tooth.

Welcome to Ella's mouth.

We have had a busy day!

Let me fill you in.

First, Ella's new alarm went off at 8 o'clock.

It went, 'Cock-a-doodle-do, cock-a-doodle-do'.

Mona the **molar** wasn't happy.

She wanted a radio alarm so she could **boogie** to music.

(Can you tell that Mona is a moaner?

Does the name give you a hint?)

I told her molars don't dance.

Their job is to crush!

Soon it was time to eat.

We chewed Ella's cereal.

Then it was time to get ready for school.

Ella brushed us.

On the way to school, Ella talked to Evan in the car.

We worked together to help Ella talk.

Teamwork makes the dream work!

At break we chewed yummy food.

Ella had an apple and carrots... CRUNCH!

After lunch, it was time for hockey.

Gary the **gumshield** came to visit.

Gary is strong. He protects us during P.E.

Today he wouldn't let me take a peek at the game.

He said it wasn't safe. Huh!

Soon it was time to go home.

Mam made chicken curry for dinner.

It was yummy!

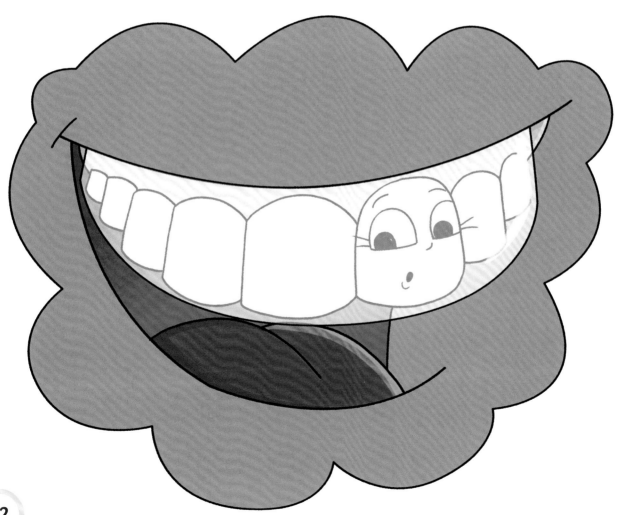

Before bed, Mona began to **complain** again.

She said she didn't feel well.

She had a pain in her root.

I told Mona she should change her name to Mac.

Maybe she wouldn't give out so much then.

This was <u>the last straw</u> for Mona.

She said she might crush me!

I hope she is better soon..."

The next morning, Ella's alarm woke her up.

"Cock-a-doodle-do, cock-a-doodle-do!"

"What a funny dream," she said.

Nana came in to see her.

Ella felt her tooth.

It didn't hurt anymore.

She told Nana the good news.

"Hurray!" said Nana.

"Mona must be feeling better," thought Ella.

She jumped out of bed.

She put on some music.

Now Mona could dance!

Ella and Nana had a dance party too.

Can you see my teeth?
I use them to chew.
I chew food like carrots,
so my teeth stay like new.

Can you see my teeth?
I use them to bite.
I bite food like apples,
so my teeth will stay white.

Can you see my teeth?
I use them to speak.
I say 't' and 'f',
every day of the week.

Can you see my teeth?
I use them to smile.
I brush until my grin
is as wide as a mile.

Saving the Library

6

Has a teacher ever told you that reading makes you smarter?

I'm sure they have.

Teachers *know* these things.

Reading **boosts** your brain power.

It's a fact.

I'm a big fan of reading.

I do it a lot.

Books about sport, space, Ireland... I read them all.

Yesterday, I read a book about Galway **hurling**.

I got the book in the library.

I visit the library all the time.

Last December, I saw a sign on the door of the library.

It said, 'Sorry, we are closing down in one month'.

"The library! Closing down?" I said to Joy the **librarian**.

"It is sad. People don't visit the library anymore," said Joy.

I walked home <u>with a heavy heart</u>.

What would I do?

I loved the library.

I learned something new every time I went.

The next day, I held a meeting.

"We have to try and save the library," said my friend Joe.

"Yes," **agreed** Grace. "The library is an important place."

All of a sudden, I had an idea.

The best way to save the library was to show it off.

If we wanted more people to come to the library... we needed to have special days in the library!

The next day, we began the Save our Library Project.

We had lots of ideas. Let me share some...

Kiss the Pig!

On Monday, Joe asked for **volunteers** to kiss his pet pig, Pork Chops.

Yes, you read that right!

First, five people put their names down.

Next, Joy got five jars and put their names on them.

Then, people put money into the jar of the person they wanted to kiss the pig.

In the end, Pat the postman was picked.

Pork Chops didn't mind.

He loved being the star.

He was <u>on the pig's back</u>!

Alice in Wonderland Tea Party

On Tuesday, Grace sold tickets to an Alice in Wonderland party.

First, she made 'Eat Me' biscuits.

There was lots of tea.

Next, you could play chess, pin the grin on the cat or paint a teacup.

Then, everyone dressed up as a **character**.

Finally, there was a quiz.

A queen of hearts and a white rabbit came to the library that day.

No one was 'late for this very important date'.

Baby Photo Contest

Me?

I held a baby photo contest on Wednesday.

It was a big **success**!

First, I asked everyone for a photo of themselves as a baby.

<u>At the drop of a hat</u>, teachers, shopkeepers and sports teams took part.

Next, lots of people came to guess who was who.

Then, they gave money and bought **raffle** tickets.

It was a great day!

After all that, our plan worked and our library stayed open. Hurray!

I hope you visit your library.

Libraries are **special**.

If you ever have a choice to read or not, **remember** the words of Dr Seuss:

> 'The more that you read,
>
> the more things you will know.
>
> The more that you learn,
>
> the more places you'll go!'

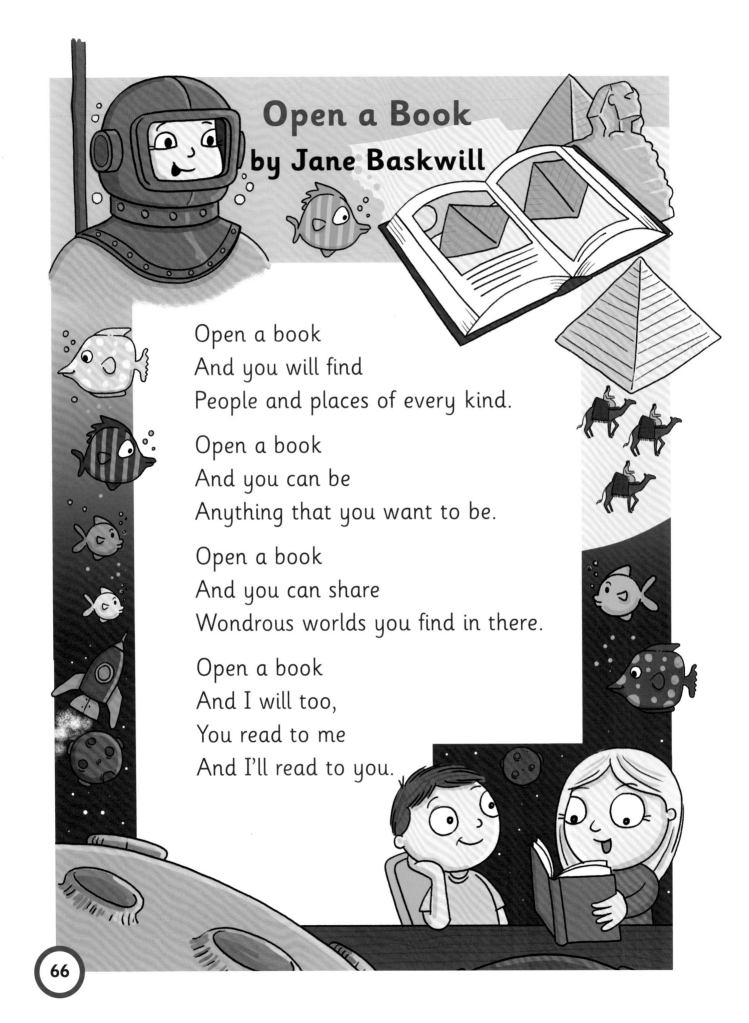

Open a Book
by Jane Baskwill

Open a book
And you will find
People and places of every kind.

Open a book
And you can be
Anything that you want to be.

Open a book
And you can share
Wondrous worlds you find in there.

Open a book
And I will too,
You read to me
And I'll read to you.

66

The Toy Show

7

My reading goal ★ Make pictures in my mind as I read.

Apply Now

Last year, the *Toy Show* was special for me.

I got ideas for my letter to Santa and I got to be on the show!

I won't <u>beat around the bush</u>, it was the BEST thing I've ever done.

Now I get to tell you all about it!

Let me begin...

In September, Mam saw an advert on the **television**.

RTÉ were looking for children to be on the *Toy Show*.

We made a video where I showed all my favourite toys.

It was a lot of fun.

Woody, Barbie and Simba were my **viewers**.

They were my biggest fans!

We sent the video to the *Toy Show*.

Then we waited… and waited… and waited.

Some weeks later, I got a letter.

I had made it to the next round! I was so excited.

I **practised** with my toys: Lego, dolls and teddies.

The next day, I went to a hotel.

There were *Toy Show* cars outside.

Children were everywhere.

Some were carrying **instruments**.

Others were dressed up.

Lots were dancing.

The hotel was a <u>hive of activity</u>!

When I got inside, a lady took my photo.

I said, "Cheese!"

Butterflies were in my tummy as I waited.

Soon my name was called.

"Good luck," **whispered** Dad.

I walked into the room.

There were five people there.

They listened to me and when I finished, they all clapped!

I was so proud.

Two weeks later, the phone rang.

I was going to be on the *Toy Show*!

Dad was so happy he did a cartwheel... and crashed into a lamp!

Soon the *Toy Show* posted me toys.

There were science kits and **experiments**.

I even got to make slime!

Some ended up on the roof. (Don't tell Mam!)

Before the show, First Class made me a good luck card.

Ms Brady said I was a **celebrity**.

On the morning of the *Toy Show*, I woke up SUPER early.

It was dark outside.

The moon was still in the sky.

I looked at it and made a wish.

Later on, I got dressed.

Mam, Dad and I went to RTÉ.

Cameras and lights were everywhere.

First, I met the host. He was funny.

Then, I saw the set. It was funky!

Next, I had a **rehearsal**. It was fantastic.

There were so many toys.

It was like a big toy shop.

Before the show began, I had time to relax.

Mam, Dad and I walked outside and saw the RTÉ Christmas lights.

They were bright and twinkly – just like me!

At last, the show began.

It was my time to shine!

I stood at my table and showed the science kits.

I marked them out of ten.

I even got to throw some slime.

Don't worry, none landed on the roof this time!

Soon, my slot was over.

The time went so fast.

Afterwards, Mam and Dad gave me a hug.

They said I was a star.

On the way home, the moon was back in the sky.

It might have even winked at me!

After all, my wish *had* come true.

The next day Mam, Dad, Meg, Mel and I looked at the *Toy Show* together.

I was so excited!

The *Toy Show* had been **streamed** all over the world.

My uncle in New York saw it.

My friend in London saw it too.

I will never forget the *Toy Show* that year.

Watch out!

Maybe next time I'll be the host.

The Toys' Playtime
By Tony Mitton

When we go to bed at the end of the day,
Our toys wake up and start to play.

They wait until we're fast asleep,
Then THEY come alive and out they creep.

The ball goes bouncing. The doll does a dance.
The little ponies preen and prance.

The toy car roars across the room.
The rocket starts to take off: ZOOM!

The robot reads a picture book,
Then teddy comes and takes a look.

And all the time we're sleeping tight,
The toys are playing through the night.

But when the sunlight warms our faces,
The toys sit quietly in their places.

They do not move. They make no noise.
You don't fool us, you naughty toys!

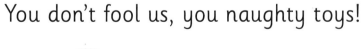

Snowed in at School

My reading goal ★ Use the sounds I know to read new words.

Wednesday began like any other day.

It was a cold winter's day.

Brrr!

We were learning about robins.

Ms Brady put a bird feeder in the **playground**.

We were **eager** to hear robins singing.

Robbie and I were putting seeds into the bird feeder when it started...

First one, then another, then another...

"IT'S SNOWING!" we shouted with **glee**.

We raced inside to tell everyone.

"Look at all the snow!" said Ms Brady.

"It's sticking," smiled Dara.

"I hope it's still there at home time," replied Robbie.

We were so excited!

All we had to do was wait for school to finish.

That turned out to be later than normal – *much* later.

After break, more snow fell.

First, it **clung** to the trees.

Then, it stuck to the grass.

Next, it hid the garden.

Our classroom felt like a snow globe.

Ms Brady got a tree and we all hung **baubles** on it.

We called it 'The Wishing Tree', because we all made a wish as we **decorated** it.

It looked so pretty.

The lights flashed blue, red, yellow and pink.

<u>To top it all off</u>, Ms Brady put on the star.

After lunch, we made Christmas cards.

Then we hung them around the room.

Christmas was on the way and we were ready for it!

Before home time, we had assembly.

Mrs Lynch **announced** the roads outside our school were closed.

I wasn't worried.

It would be fun to walk home in the snow!

Then Mrs Lynch said we had to stay in school longer than normal.

People couldn't travel in the snowstorm.

Everyone had to wait until the snow stopped.

That was when I knew I was snowed in at school.

After assembly, we went back to our classroom.

The bell rang for home time, but nobody left.

First, we **decided** to watch a movie.

Ms Brady turned our classroom into a cinema.

We rolled out the mats from the P.E. hall and got **comfortable**.

We watched *The Polar Express*.

Tom fell asleep – no surprises there!

(Sometimes I called him Aurora, just like Sleeping Beauty.

But <u>don't let the cat out of the bag</u> and tell him... I don't think he'd be happy with me!)

During the movie, Ms Brady gave us some popcorn. It was yummy.

Later on, Ms Brady read *The Witches* aloud.

I <u>was all ears</u> when Ms Brady read, **especially** as it was by Roald Dahl.

She was a great **actress** and used lots of silly voices.

She even wore a witch's hat.

When Ms Brady read, <u>we hung onto every word</u>.

Next, we put on a show.

It was called 'First Class Has Got Talent!'

Everyone took part.

Alex did some magic tricks.

Lainey sang a rap.

Dara sang a song, but forgot the words halfway through, so he told some jokes instead.

Here is one of them: What do elves eat for breakfast?

Snow-flakes!

Before it got dark outside, it stopped snowing.

We wrapped up and *finally* left the classroom.

We had the best time ever outside.

We had a snowball fight and made snow angels.

Everyone in First Class helped build a snowman, even Ms Brady!

We all stood beside our snowman so that Mrs Lynch could take a photo.

Click!

The icing on the cake was when Dad came to pick me up.

The **council** had cleared the road.

Three hours later than planned, I finally left school.

I had a brilliant snow day in school.

It was so much fun!

It took a few days for the snow to melt.

When we went back to school, Ms Brady stuck our snowman photo on the wall.

She said, "This photo will help us remember our snow day."

But I didn't need a photo.

I knew I could *never* forget being snowed in at school!

When Santa Claus Comes

A good time is coming, I wish it were here,
The very best time in the whole of the year;

I'm counting each day on my fingers and thumbs –
the weeks that must pass before Santa Claus comes.

Then when the first snowflakes begin to come down,
And the wind whistles sharp and the branches are brown,

I'll not mind the cold, though my fingers it numbs,
For it brings the time nearer when Santa Claus comes.

New Year, New Visitors

My reading goal ★ Predict what will happen next in this story.

Tom always liked the first day of the New Year.

This year he liked the New Year more than ever!

It all began when Grandad Kelly and Tom went to Dublin Airport.

Tom LOVED the airport.

People rushed around with their bags and **passports**.

The excitement of going somewhere new hung in the air.

Grandad said, "Happy New Year!" to *everyone* he met.

Tom thought Grandad must have *very* high hopes for the New Year.

Maybe this was the year Roscommon would win the All Ireland!

Or maybe this year Grandad would finally finish building his shed.

That would please Nana.

87

They had come to the airport to meet Tom's **cousin** Jude and his family.

They were travelling from New Zealand.

It was very far away.

That morning, Tom and Luna looked up New Zealand on the map.

"Wouldn't it be cool to travel there some day?" Tom asked.

"Woof," replied Luna.

Tom thought he saw Luna nodding her head.

"It would be woof-tastic," he imagined her saying.

Dogs are so clever!

In the airport, Tom and Grandad waited for their **visitors**.

Tom had <u>ants in his pants</u>.

It had been a long time since Jude was last home.

They had both been babies.

Tom saw Grandad hopping from one foot to the other.

Hop, hop, hop went his feet.

Tom thought Grandad was dancing.

They were so excited, they could not stand still!

Soon, Tom saw Jude and his family.

Tom and Jude ran to each other.

Jude gave Tom a big hug.

"Guess what, Tom?" said Jude. "We've **travelled** halfway around the world and we have no bags!"

"Our bags got lost," Jude's dad explained.

At least that's what Tom *thought* he said.

It was hard to hear him, because Grandad kept saying "Happy New Year" over and over again!

"We don't know when they're going to get to Ireland. Mam's worried," said Jude.

Normally, missing bags would be OK. A **nuisance**, but not a big deal.

The problem was Jude had a nut **allergy**.

His suitcase had **medicine** and nut-free snacks inside.

"Don't worry," said Grandad. "Your suitcase will get here soon."

"Fingers crossed," replied Jude.

Over the next few days, Jude and Tom had a super time.

They saw <u>eye to eye</u> right away.

They were like twins, because Jude wore Tom's clothes.

They went to the Cliffs of Moher to see where the *Harry Potter* movie was filmed.

Tayto Park was great fun too.

The zip lines were the best.

It felt like they were flying!

When it came to food, Tom and Jude's parents came to the rescue.

They baked snacks that had zero nuts or nut **traces** in them.

Pancakes, bars, muffins... they made lots of food!

Every time they ate in a **restaurant**, Jude's parents made sure his food was free from nuts.

They told the waiters about Jude's allergy and packed lots of food for him to eat.

A few days later, the airport rang.

"Our bags have made it to Ireland," announced Jude's dad.

"Woohoo!" said Jude.

Grandad went to the airport to collect the suitcases.

They had taken a trip to Australia.

"They must have had a fantastic time!" laughed Grandad. "Maybe I'll try to squeeze into your suitcase on the way back! I'd like to visit the land down under."

Jude and Tom imagined Grandad **squished** up inside a suitcase and began to laugh.

"It's great you have your favourite snacks, Jude," said Tom.

"Even better, I can give you your presents now," replied Jude.

He gave Tom a kiwi teddy and a rugby jersey. Luna even got a bone!

Everyone enjoyed the rest of the holiday.

Tom was already planning a trip to New Zealand.

How **incredible** would that be?

He just hoped his bags wouldn't go on holidays without him!

The Best of Friends
by Jill Wolf

The best of friends,
Can change a frown,
Into a smile,
When you feel down.

The best of friends,
Will understand,
Your little trials,
And lend a hand.

The best of friends,
Will always share,
Your secret dreams,
Because they care.

The best of friends,
Worth more than gold,
Give all the love,
A heart can hold.